Thank you for all your understanding and support.

Author:

A simple fellow soul who believes in, completely rational, eternal, and heavenly happiness can be plausible for all. Starting from You!

Irrespective of who we are, it would greatly help us understand the most Reasonable and the most Useful divine concepts like Soul. Importantly reap benefits of it personally and for all.

We all seek for, more blissful, meaningful, reliable, and sustainable everyday life, starting from our own self. Understanding of the commonly misunderstood and unclear relationships among all the existences provides us greatly profound functional wisdom. Logically, it could also be the simplest path for Exponential Pleasure for all.

Reasonable and pure Goodness is Eternal! All the Souls, knowingly and unknowingly, seek for the Eternal Happiness!

Every day we make numerous decisions on various solutions towards seeking and solving problems. It could be personal, social, professional, small or big, or any number of sorts of problems. In the end, irrespective of any of our beliefs and deeds, it should settle in expected or unexpected. In fact, Any Outcomes that initially that cannot be Known.

Anything considerable we do could lead to search for one or more solutions. It could be one attempt, or many attempts to solve a problem successfully. Sometimes it could be endless attempts to solve a problem, still without a sensible, significant, substantial, and sustainable resolution.

In simple, for better solutions, we should ask ourselves some important questions.

Like, Are we looking at all the important Facts and Resources?

Are we communicating Explicitly, and confirming the Understanding with realistic expectations. Primarily and essentially as unclear communication could lead to Utter Failures that supposed to be Completely Thriving Success?

Are we ALL participating and contributing realistically?

Are we using the most Reasoning timely possible?

Are we receiving Reliable outcomes, even if minimally, progressively?

Are we creating solutions that can be factually Verified and Sustained?

Are we truly Learning and implementing consistently?

Are we trying to framework Compassionately equitable, Comprehensively streamlined, Sincerely strategic, and further more. All in the end, meaningfully and dependably help All.

When we attempt to solve a problem with Complete Inclusivity in as many aspects as reasonably possible, we could create thriving Solutions. When we focus on Completeness, better understanding of Souls could be vital. It would lead us to creating best of the Sustainable solutions. Essentially as it would benefit, praise, raise, and include All involved. Significantly because it would be Willingly, and especially Respectfully inclusive.

Briefly, when we believe in Soul Solutions and act on, it would greatly benefit. In simple, it would be by Respecting and Offering Reasonable Goodness for all, and Rationally Requiring the same from all involved. When it is followed consistently, it would lead to lasting success, peace and pleasure for all.

It is about every single individual's happiness starting from our own

self. We could achieve More Goodness Harmoniously, even at times, if it is not that obvious for us. When thoughtfully analyzed and recognized, it would be apparent that we would undoubtedly receive More Consequential Happiness. Profoundly, it would be instantly and over time.

We all desire, pray for, and produce goodness, at our own levels. It is also for lasting contentment, for now and for ever. It is great. At the same time, we might need to try it some more reasonably and realistically.

Some of us might ask, How can we even define Goodness as it could differ for different people and groups? Correct, it is not easy! Well, for true, it might meaningfully, mutually and beneficially take considerable efforts. We could focus on facts, outcomes, pros and cons so far. In its completeness, and work on it as a group, we would find out more and more gradually, about True Goodness.

Especially, we must start try to practice it, whenever and wherever plausible. In numerous aspects, it would directly and indirectly, make our own lives more in peace and pleasurable.

At any level feasible, we must try to attain Complete Goodness - given the circumstances. Importantly then on, carry it afterwards equitably. We must rationally help each other as we are helping our own selves. Naturally or at least for our own Unexplainable Soul's Goodness that Pushes for the Hidden Eternal Happiness.

It is a journey. We must attempt to properly realize and understand. If we do so, for even small Goodness we produce, we forward ourselves to further True Inner Joy. That we cannot even conceive or articulate.

Along the way, we might even make some mistakes. Unfortunately and unknowingly some sins too. For reliable happiness, that need not stop the Soul's - Goodness Journey. Consciously, recognize the mistakes, forgive yourself, request for forgiveness, correct rationally, and move on.

Wisely, steadily, and consistently, we would start creating more and more Goodness. If we could, we would relish completely cheerful, sustainable, and heavenly happiness. Such great pleasure would be, for this life and beyond - if you believe in it.

We have got All and Beyond to create such blissful state. But the *willingness* of those souls that feasibly can. Also, the contribution of ALL involved, sensibly with No Exceptions. This would accomplish the state of Conclusive Truth - Remarkably Phenomenal and Timeless Happiness.

When it transpires, it would be YOU the first to relish the true joyfulness. As you are the one in this conversation, and willing to do the best for yourself. Along with you everyone will join you harmoniously. It is completely feasible.

End of the Soul Solution Search for reasonable common problems and sufferings. The Dawn of the Complete Eternal Bliss for All - Starting from You!

Thank you! Have a Great Day-Every Day!

Sincerely - A Fellow Soul,
Somu Sivaramakrishnan

CONTENTS

Prologue

Welcome and Thank you for joining me in this Conversation! In this short journey with a fellow-soul, let's mutually find out, how a completely reasonable, harmonious, goodness, and happiness filled life can be real and plausible. Not just for Us, but for All Souls, Irrespective of any of our current believes. **Especially, in a profound way, observe, discover, realize, and enjoy that you are the most valuable soul that exists.** Who also deserves the most blissful happiness - in a very profound and positive way.

"Really?!"

I think so! Let's briefly explore!

Well! The exceptionally uninvited wander - when in it. Wondering the very existence - when walk it. It could be a blessing - when done it. The overwhelming that you strive to overcome, over and over that led to this Soul Solution Search journey.

Especially, resolve to critical problems. An attempt, for making the soul's walk-the-walk, in this life and plausibly beyond - a pleasant good fortune! When received, such consistently evolving extreme opportunities, revealed Patterns that could alleviate and resolve.

They are the Reasonable Patterns that could produce best of the solutions, for all the problems.

Initially it may not be evident. Though, it would resolve for every single problem that we face every day. **More reasonably - at least for the most problems that we face, the most reasonable, rewarding, and harmonious solutions exist.** Notably, it benefits the entirety. This peaceful and pleasureful state can be achieved by Promoting, Reliable and Rational Goodness that Sustains.

In brief, the patterns recommend that all starts from individuals and their own seeking for happiness. Irrespective of the numerous believes that we may have, if we are not here, it would make no sense at all. Assume, if we are not here, we would not even know or realize, the existence of anything here, or anywhere.

Our existence is the most important and our own happiness is the paramount for each of us. How we achieve such, possibly sustainable happiness, could differ among us. Still YOU are the most important in this short journey. Right here and right now, you are the one who could deserve the very bests of the eternal bliss - tangibly and profoundly!

Structure of the Book

In this book of, 'Soul Solution Search Series - 101 to 777! Discussion and Solution on common complex questions!', this is Edition 1. A Short TOPIC Book, that converses on "God".

These series of books on 'Soul Solution Search' would be released like this Short TOPIC Books. Also, there would be Combined-TOPICS Books that would speak on various topics. This would be for more and better understanding of the Soul's eternal journey.

Each Topic would start with adequate level of introduction. Where appropriate, also some of common questions, answers and reasonable solutions would be discussed. The contents may start at simple levels, so that it would be easy for the common readers. The conversation would evolve from there. Further, it would grow based on the flow, needs, interests received, and beyond. Each Edition would be expanded with appropriate and considerably enriched contents.

For Readers who may be interested in Specific TOPIC, separate 'Short TOPIC Book' would be released. These Short TOPIC Books will have some of common conversations, and specific substance furnished for better understanding.

Primary Sources of the Contents

Contents of these Series of Books are primarily based on the vast extra ordinary personal experiences and opportunities that I received. They are both wonderfully also blissfully great, and terribly also awfully bad experiences. I am very Thankful for all the wealth of experiences. Though, I greatly prefer those that make the situation better for all involved. More importantly, Self motivated Soul Solution Search for specific problems, and self-interpretations of everyday wisdom from all fellow-souls like you. My heartily honor, appreciation, and Thanks for that. Thank you!

Further, if anyone finds any of the content as inappropriate in anyways, please forgive me. Please note that the intent of the content is to promote Reasonable, Sustainable, Completely Inclusive - Goodness based Happiness for All.

Acknowledgements

*Thanks for my **Parents** for bringing me to this Great World,*
*Thanks for my Great **Friends** for teaching me to Think Good,*
*Thanks for my **Family** for their extended support during Toughest Times,*
*and **Special Thanks for You** for accompanying me in this Brief Journey!*

Further, I would like to extend my Thanks for those who unknowingly hurt me! I pray for their souls also! I Thank them because, as those who did Right for me Taught me how to be Good like them, those who did wrong to me Taught me how I should not be! It's an important learning that made me to Search for Good Solutions and Answers. I believe, that made me a better Soul. They are very vital part of the truth and the Journey of the Souls! I wish that they realize and correct me and correct themselves! So, I Thank them!

Additionally, my Thanks for Everyone, Everything and Nothing - All the Souls!

❖꧁꧁꧁꧁꧁꧁꧁❋꧂꧂꧂꧂꧂꧂꧂❖

God

Based on common intelligence and Rational thoughts, I believe that God must exists, irrespective of anyone believes it or not. It would be similar to, wind exists not because everyone and everything that breathes it Believes in it. Also able to make sure of its existence all the times. But because, just it is the way it is - Profound Nature!

Naturally, as part of evolution, the concept of the God exists for thousands of years. Everything evolves over time! and so our understanding of God!

In general, evolution happens both in beneficial - rightful ways, and harmful - wrongful ways. The beneficial - rightful ways generally, evolve starting with Reasoning, and slowly Sustainably.

Irrespective of any of our personal believes, either naturally or otherwise, things happen that we do not have complete understanding. Many times, not complete, but not even rational understanding of things, as with no clear explanation, and also no clear proof.

Rationally, we should assume that they still evolve. So, a more clear understanding of God that could benefit all, with out any exceptions, is still evolving!

For each of us and our Souls, we do not rationally remember, if we believed to be born. But we were born, and we are living our lives. Similarly, our lives end - when it supposed to be, all is done for each of us in this life. Our lives, apparently happened to start, and should obviously happen to end. It happens without much of our own Known and Careful control.

We may know some, even profound details, as we have evolved to the current intelligent beings so far identified. But still, the profound understanding of lives, and countless other things, yet to be far better understood. It seems a very long and eternal way to go.

The existence of God is felt and meaningfully understood, in numerously different ways by countless souls. Even though, with more complete details, expectations, proof, and wisdom, tangibly with Complete Reasoning yet to be proved.

Please know that I BELIEVE in God. I Only BELIEVE, and HAPPILY, based on my own interpretations, expectations, and following - in a fruitful way for all! Still long way to go!

Sure, this is the era of, so far, the most human advancements - in our own words, expectations, and understanding. Especially, so far known, not just on our Earth, but also in this entire Universe!

We are Not Sure, if there are already Transcended Surreal around us on this earth. May be somewhere in the vast unimaginable Universe, that we yet to find. As currently we cannot see, identify, analyze, and recognize.

Essentially, if we could find, still we would analyze, with our own definition. Such as, what is a living life form as we know it, and ways and foundation for Beliefs. Obviously, this would be based on, our own experience and knowledge from these past few thousands of years.

We have at least thousands of years of our various Beliefs being followed. Further, our current exponential and unprecedented advancements achieved.

Do we have clear understanding on the purpose, foundation, and clear framework for appropriate use of such profound beliefs?

I believe, we need further more learning and understanding to complete, for true benefits.

Consider our history on various things, and astonishing successes in them. Can we compare it with our progress on various profound beliefs? Reasonably, and clearly, we are Not successful in many of our profound Beliefs. At least, not so far!

This is even after based on, all the tools and opportunities that we have developed all along. They could have profoundly assisted to a sustainable success for our Kind the Human Kind. At least to start with, in many of our profound beliefs.

Currently, we are Racing for something that we do not have clear understanding of. Human Race in many ways, has long way to become a truly blissful Human Kind. Such truly thriving Human Kind with

profound understanding, reasonable beliefs, and implementable frameworks would produce sustainable happiness for the entirety.

Assume, if other beings and even non-beings have Profound and Beneficial Beliefs that we yet to find out and understand.

Rationally Inconceivable! Just assume, if such exists that is unknown or unidentified for now. Also if they are able to use it, in a thoughtful way, for their True Eternal Paradise!

Would we know, if any such Beings are able to Think, Thank, and Devote truly beneficially. In their own ways for their Creator? Not serious - Just assumption! May be we are not able to imagine, but further profoundly even Non-beings. It would be hard to conceive, as we define 'Rational' based on our own understanding. Can they do so?!

We may know some about our pets, and such beings that are loving, or useful, or threatening, or simply some in general. We may know, how to feed them, behave with them, their physical anatomy. Especially, how to control them, and such.

We do not know much about, if they have any profound beliefs that would sensibly enrich them as a whole. If so, would they ornament their most appreciation, by offering their True Goodness for their Kinds. As outcome, try to and able to, Live Eternally Happily?! We just have no such knowledge.

"What? It must be impossible!". I agree! Human Race is superior in countless ways.

But the fact of the matter is, We Don't Know! So far, after extreme and profound hard work of countless souls, we have considerable findings about other species. We had identified and documented with reasonable details, for about 5 to 10 million species on Earth. Truly Great, but could be far from complete. There could be billions, even more, we do not know.

How about the countless questions we have and we would have for ages to come in the Whole Universe?!

Our Science, Technologies and such advancements bring us unimaginable and implausible evolution. These cannot even be comprehended by any one human being. But comparing to that, the unknown for human beings in this Universe, could be inconceivably far beyond that.

Thanks for all the Great souls for their hard work, innovation, and progress. But, all our advancements could relatively are very little, with respect to True Knowledge and Success! It might not be simple, but as evident, so far, we could not build a reasonably successful human kind.

If not, a Completely Blissful and Harmonious world, at least, a world with Reasonable and Sustainable framework. Plausibly poverty free, suffering free, war free, deceives free, disease free world, without the numerous further terrible troubles.

At least, How about **a Model for Sustainable Economy for All The Human Kind. It would use tools, techniques, strategies, and advancements of Computers, Mega machines, Robots, Artificial Intelligence and more?!**

In brief, all the basic needs are available for all. In fact, this could be the best Economic Model that we ever created. Today, with complete reasoning, and all our current innovations, it must be plausible.

Now, we are with so much true sophistication, honestly superior, and ever pioneering tools. Also, alongside, enormous loads of gizmos. Positively, these are our basis for tomorrow. The exponential evolution to come that cannot even be predicted for now.

It is apparent that, the current progression of our Human Race Now, is Remarkably Incomparable to the Past. Presume, we reached such even further beyond, Blessed Futuristic Advancements.

Are we sure, to Rationally and Sustainably utilize. Especially, employ such blissfulness to our True Progress?

I am not very sure. Because, in many important ways, so far, we were not able to utilize our advancements. By now, we should have truly and sustainably produced a Rational State of Results. Predictably, still we are in the beginning of this eternal voyage!

In brief, even though we - the human kind have accomplished so much. Still the unknown to understand and achieve, is far beyond our own imaginations.

In some aspects, we are mostly, overly proud infants and babies, relatively comparing to the Completeness! I am one of them!

I believe that we had been given so much by the God. If you want to call Nature or Evolution. We, as a whole, need to learn, to make a better world for ourselves.

So, if we do not have complete understanding, or do not have proof that if there is God or not. I think that is okay.

When we are here, we just want to live to the fullest happiest life, for all, helping each other. I believe it must be plausible.

By the understanding of the profound souls, God represents complete Goodness and complete Happiness.

God cannot be Deceived.

The wealth of God possesses complete knowledge. Inconceivable, but to the sub-atomic level details, and sub-cellular level feelings and emotions!

Helps especially the Good ones, and Supports the Bad to become Good.

For all, Teaches Better things.

Has complete control over anything and everything that ever existed or conceived. But purposefully, does not interfere with the Profound Freewill.

God offers opportunities for us, to recover our souls from the mistakes and sins. That we may have made, knowingly or unknowingly.

Helps us reach Heaven.

God forgives our mistakes, and where applicable also our sins.

God has complete factual knowledge of everything that happened and happens. At an unimaginable abundance of enormity.

Judges ALL with Completely Reasonable Wisdom that no one and nothing can mislead.

Please note that we are trying to discuss here with a constructive and complimentary attitude. If we think about God or such of our thoughtful believes, the underlying framework would favorably support. It would be in our, all kinds of everyday deeds. Especially because, they have practical and immeasurable domino effects. It cannot even be contemplated.

Ultimately, if we could follow the goodness rationally, may be with some understandable mistakes. We would be in complete peace, of course, with reasonable and obvious, minimal sufferings. That will fulfill the eternal completeness, as might be conceivably found in the Heavens. Further, under the complete justice of the eternal blissfulness, for our own selves and for all.

We have been given the most precious gift of all - The Unprecedented Intelligence. Unimaginable hard work brought us where we are. Filled with greatest tools that could help us reach the eternal happiness.

It is apparent that we have the blessings of the divinity! Do we have the *Willingness,* to do the right for ourselves?!

We are here to wake up, wander, walk and reach - the fundamental framework, for a Truly Blessed Human Kind! If we could reach there, then our Creator - God, The Almighty or any of our Divine Beliefs, would bless us all.

We all would have a Truly Sustainable, Meaningful, Purposeful and Blissful Life.

How do you know, if there is God?

I feel the Goodness of the God through everyday experiences. It does not mean that it is only, and completely happiness filled. Even if I feel such complete happiness always, it is not going to answer the question. As it's my own feelings and interpretations, and not anything tangible for you.

Please note that if someone does not believe in God. Even if I show something, that seems to be tangible. It might be called as magic, among other interpretations.

Among other profound reasons, in simple, I believe in God. Like the millions and billions of Good Souls, who try to make some Common Good out of it. Further, it is also very important for me to be Thankful for God. For anything and everything Good that I received.

In brief, assume an atom or another smallest particle that we could define. To move it from point A to point B. May be the shortest distance that we could conceive and measure. However smallest it could be. It would still require some minimal energy or a force to move it.

We evidence, countless things that we encounter in our lifetime. Either realized or not. For lack of terms, there must be enormous wisdom and energy that must support it. This would be without bothering the cumulative freewill of all the existences. Some call it nature, some call it 'that is the way it is', without a name. I call its part of 'God', like the billions. You may call it as one of it, or something completely different.

In the end, for Profound Benefits, it is very important to understand and recognize. The Presence of, something very fundamental and very important. The existence of someone or something far beyond our own selves. Infinite Knowledge and experience, that we are not able to even conceive.

In simple, I feel and know that there is God! If someone further is doubtful, and emphasize more and more. It could also be for a different answer or further profound reasons. So, I may be tending to tell something more rational that may comfort them better. It would be to keep the situation in peace. Even though, I would realize that it is not how I feel about it!

I could argue and emphasize with examples and more on my beliefs. At the same time, I also believe. Not to overly emphasize on my own beliefs, feelings and interpretations.

Especially where it is not welcome or might create unnecessary conflicts. May also simply, hurt the feelings of the others with whom I discuss. It just feels not necessary and not correct.

Please note that. Any of such thoughtful beliefs, and if it has any meaning to, it would reveal its complete truth. More importantly, for it, when appropriate circumstances occur. It would be either in this obvious life, or the beyond eternal life. Again if you believe in it!

What is the proof that God exists?

There are various incidents throughout the history, where some Great Souls did miracles. Some believed, some others did not believe. There are such events happen even these days. No questions, there are plenty of Goodness exists in this world! At the same time, if you encounter one such, just beware of fakes, aware and make sure of the ultimate Goodness it is to offer. Also it will happen in the days, years, and millennia to come.

Great, if such miracles happen that you could witness! But, if God must be proved, only through something tangible, or such means. Then we are taking a chance to be deceived by some who could perform great magic. They might try to deceive and receive, what they want to wrongfully achieve from it.

If you do not believe in God, just reasonably do not be bothered by it. Who knows, when you could get a personal experience to make you feel and believe in God for yourselves.

If Science wants proof of God, think about the birth of the Universe that happened about 14 billion years ago! How can it be proved at all in a tangible and practical way to a common person?! The Earth was created about 4 billion years ago! Which Time Machine would we take to witness this supposed to be fact?!

There are countless things Science wants us to believe in that have no meaningful and experiential proof. Like, if we travel million light years away! It is not Science's fault! Still we believe in it, because this is the best of the knowledge we have got, so far. I believe in them.

The fact of the matter is, for a reasonably intelligent soul. The purpose of the belief on 'God' is, not to be proved. But to be felt, understood, and used, as a Profound Gift. To be progressively evolved, and relished through. It is the understanding of, the ability to achieve,

Reasonable Common Goodness and Sustainable Happiness for all. It would be through, such supremely meaningful belief to offer - the Complete Bliss.

What if someone believes in something different than mine, or do destructive deeds?

Honestly, please do not be annoyed or angered, just because, someone believes in something different than what you believe in! In fact, like your good beliefs and feelings. It may also be the same kind of feeling the other one may also have. Just minimum pretend and treat gently, how you want to be treated, in such a scenario. Who knows, that other person or group could be a wonderful soul. That could become your best friend or an associate, and save your life someday somewhere!

Accept or forget! No need to argue or fight. Especially, in a wrongful direction, for something that we do not even have complete understanding about. When there is a chance for violence. No true God would want you to argue or fight to prove something and put yourself in harms way. So, please move forward with your own best beliefs - in a friendly way.

Whatever happened in the past, and whatever to come going forward. Now we have millennia of reasoning and understanding. In a meaningful way, anything and everything related to God - only means and spreads constructive, soothing and pleasing outcomes for all. Nothing destructive!

If you find outcomes of such belief, as you rationally feel and evidently recognize leading to anything destructive. For sure, that must not be about 'God'. In that situation, the belief is simply used as an excuse, for the bad deeds committed to harm. It is nothing to do with the underlying belief itself.

Be aware, do the needful, and move on to peace. Proceed to more rational circumstances where you will find much reasoning, kindness, harmony, and bliss. That is what your Good God would want for you and for all.

If there is God as most people believe, why bad in the world?! What is the Solution to correct the situation?!

Great Souls pray for Thanking God. Also for everyone's and everything's Happiness. Further, of course also for their own needs and then wants. Clever at the same time Good Souls, first, pray for their own needs and wants. Then they would pray for the other souls. There is nothing wrong in it!

Most of the people just physically pray God. Mostly for their own wants. May also be for some common Good, that sometimes benefit them in turn as well. Again, nothing wrong!

Further, some self-centered individuals and groups that when leave the prayer hall of any sort. Also leave back there, their basic reasoning, empathy, ethics, and Goodness. When they are at their business, at work or wherever and whatever they do. They completely forget about the simple, "Cannot deceive God! God knows it all!". As outcome, they do less than standard - simply greedy to extremely inhumane deeds. It affects the common Good in unimaginable-fundamental ways. I feel sorry for their souls as well. As it is not all their own wrongful deeds.

These basically greedy and bad intentioned individuals and groups justify to themselves that they are not that bad. This is based on their own understanding, and their own interpretation, on their own deeds. Again, it is bad. But it is not just completely their own fault.

From their perspective, they are just being flexible to fit the needs. Such as, to survive in the tough world, and use excuses to cover up their bad. They may say, "for the survival in the doggy-dog (dog-eat-dog) world", "nice finish last, so just I am being clever", etc.

They seem to completely ignore that the God they apparently prayed in one or the other means and ways, knows them completely. Every single thought, word, deed, consequences, and the inconceivable Domino Effects they caused in wrongful and harmful ways.

Looking at historically and analyzing reasonably. It seems that these unfortunate and wrongful souls, unknowingly and knowingly, do some bad. Then request for forgiveness, and wait for if are punished. **Because of its deepest profoundness. The divine Forgiveness and punishment does Not Always occur, based on our own current understanding.**

When they are not punished apparently for their bad. Instead of Thanking their God, for not punishing them, and giving them the opportunity to correct. They do not correct their deeds by themselves. Not quite understanding the profound divinity. Some of them, seem to continue do further bad in more aggressive ways.

In this case, they totally rejected to understand the Goodness and true Gift. Their beloved God's heavenly forgiveness, and the opportunity to correct.

They seem to disregard the significance, magnitude, and the multifaceted foundation of Freewill.

They missed a great chance of the exponentially glorious and self beneficial - self enrichment. Towards more reasoning, self realization of their bad deeds, and become one of truly forgiven Souls.

Their further wrongful behaviors also fueled by their greed on materialistic wealth. Also raise in their social status, and more such impermanent temptations.

Unfortunately, This Time around they failed, not those, they deceived. But more importantly, Themselves Awfully!

They are unable to and unwilling to understand the reason for the God's gift of many great opportunities - This Time - To Test Them.

Still from their own perspective they respect God through their prayers and offerings to God or Charities, etc. Further sensibly, they could remove their sins and mistakes through various reasonable and tangible Good means gradually! Also, along the way, they could produce meaningful Goodness wherever plausible, and when they wish for also sometimes accidentally - even that counts!

Some of the concepts and beliefs about God of sinful souls could be profound and true. Sincerely and tangibly they need to work on it. If not, either in this life, or beyond, unfortunately they must pay for it in big. Before they could realize, learn, and thrive. In general, there would be countless opportunities to avoid the coming around sufferings. The best is to do, as much Good as plausible, when any and all chances come across.

When the sinful had opportunities to do things right, unfortunately 'they chose to do bad with their own freewill'. Most of the times, they do not realize one important thing. **By doing bad, they did the Worst for Their Own Soul. Also in certain ways, those related Good souls that they care for any reason. Not Just for it, but also the harmful**

domino effects that they unknowingly caused. More Specifically that could incrementally affect countless, for a very long time to come. All these could completely have been avoided.

If Nothing Done To Resolve it, those harmful deeds and outcomes, follow them wherever their soul should go. That no one tangibly knows. But mostly they would get chances, to Not Just overcome. But go beyond and attain complete peace and pleasure. Provided they utilize it!

Many of such sinful souls do not utilize the opportunities when they could. In the end, in their death bed they suffer. Then they might not have sufficient energy to even support themselves or even to breath. At that time, they cry and beg for forgiveness. Hopefully, their soul would at least have some benefits for any of their true realization. Unless no other options, just meaningless sympathy alone would do little good.

At that time, no one, and especially no God want them to be fearful, cry, scream and hurt themselves. Positively and hopefully, they are forgiven by the Graceful God! At least, they must start thinking and doing Good Reasonably and Faithfully from then on.

God represents Complete Grace, Comfort and Goodness. Doing Reasonable Good at whatever level possible would help. They could remove sufferings of their sin, receive God's blessing, in profound and practical ways.

There is vast level of misunderstanding exists on forgiveness. In brief, if one did bad, forgiveness will Not Alone Help. The Reason with also plausible resolutions, are discussed more deeply in the Forgiveness Shortbook.

More grace - more opportunities - if used it Wisely! Until death, there are more opportunities that all Souls could use. Bad souls, even at the death bed, could do some Reasonable Good. It would offer more relief.

In addition to the received forgiveness, doing the most Good is important. Especially, helping those, who were put to suffer. It would truly enable, and make feel the heaven on this earth. It would be right then, as apparent relief from the sins. This relief would be for now and eternal. Continue helping any sensible Good souls around, would greatly enrich the bliss.

Towards end of the life and such situations, fearful aggressions would not produce meaningful results. Doing any Good, even pleasant Good thoughts for those made to suffer would benefit. In addition, praying for forgiveness would produce much true comfort and peace.

When doing any good feasible, who knows how long the newly found Goodness and pleasure can fortunately extend. It could even bloom to a paradise on the earth. Unfortunately, if it is further too late and continued, may lead to meaningless suffering!

Even if nothing is possible, at least, simple, rational, Good prayers will make the sinful forget harmful thoughts. It would also bring more calming, soothing and relief for themselves. More importantly, people around.

In simple, Prayers help self emphasize the most important things for us. If such prayers involve more common Goodness, it can also create greater pleasures. In brief, it is a great tool that makes our souls and minds focus on what is more important for us. It is up to us. We could do good for ourselves and plausibly all around us, with this greatly blessed practice.

Further, it would be great, to pray and do some more mindful Common Good. It could gradually and drastically improve our own every day life significantly. It would improve common standards of livings, inner peace, own safety around, enriched quality of living, and more. In simple, it gives opportunities for more sensible pleasures. All as awards for the simple Common Goodness produced.

When we pray for more Lucid Goodness, we teach and practice our inner souls. Practicing to think, talk, and do more Good. Such gradual perfecting would ultimately extend more pleasure. Further, bring more meaning and peace - principally when needed.

This is because the **heartfelt Prayers would evolve to be Good Thinking, Pleasant Speaking, and ultimately Great Deeds. Flourish the Deeper Inner Soul!**

Great and Good Souls, enjoy their spiritual being. They speak with God like speaking with their own Good parents or Loving Soul mate or True friends. This would be irrespective of their current other aspects and constraints. Such as, their past, financial circumstances, health conditions, social status they are in, and many more.

Irrespective of who they are, the most blessed, would have all the bliss within them. This would be, even with little. Such true joyfulness, cannot be materially recognized, rationally related, conceivably articulated or evidently understood. That is the miracle of the Goodness that was and still is being produced!

Some Great Souls, who are under severe 'Tests', may have constraints and immense sufferings. But still their inner Souls would feel profound happiness that could not be explained. Subtle God's Grace! At reasonable conditions, they would realize very pleasant experience. This would be with their overall self, present life, inner confidence and feel the simple but true blissfulness. It would feel more than just a wonderful day dream. But true enriched pleasure presently. Further genuine envision for the inconceivably eternal after life.

In brief, God forgives with all holiness without constraints - through opportunities to correct! It is not part of the Forgiveness By Itself to remove the sin. It has to be earned. Such gift of opportunities, properly, to be utilized, to wash off the sins by themselves. One's own thoughts, deeds and consequences shall ultimately shape up and go along with them. Finally, for the judgment, all in full would go, as Karma or any other beliefs.

So, God as either believed or conceived, without Good understanding, is Not the reason for any bad in the world. I believe, you have asked this thoughtful question. You might also believe and accept the concept of 'Freewill' that God does not affect.

If thoroughly learned and understood, 'God' however practiced tries to help towards Peace, Goodness and Happiness for all. If not, however called, it may not be about 'God' that we are discussing.

Unfortunately bad exists, because the bad deeds of the thoughtless souls involved that yet to evolve noticeably. Not anything to do with the belief on God! Like discussed above, there are many simple resolutions exist to resolve it. Including truthful prayers.

Further, more important, practical, well analyzed and thought through solutions can be implemented broadly. When implemented correctly, it would help the faith and profound beliefs. It would be substantial, sustainable, splendorous paradigm shift. For the entire human kind, and beyond.

These are few, vitally important and exponentially beneficial for all. It would be predominant and fruitful. Because the world is asking for, more and more reasons in the recent past. That is unlike, the thousands of years of beliefs, mainly based on following.

As first step, a few simple and most important changes can be made. Though the solution may seem simple, the implementation could require considerable efforts.

It would be through beneficial thoughtful conversations, and fundamental enabling. More importantly, the understanding of the Great Benefits these ideas to offer.

Especially, in this era, there are many unreasonable and harmful followings. Large portions of the human kind, is moving completely away from

ANY kind of faith. Unfortunately, people do not have faith in, peace and pleasure in the world for all. Including faith in themselves.

Sustainability in mind, for example, we need to rephrase a few words, without upset of the core principles and faith. For example, the use of, "Only"! For instance, "This is the ONLY way to reach Heaven", "This is the ONLY God", "This is the ONLY Group to achieve", "This is the ONLY Way to achieve ", and so on. When used it correctly by all with thorough understanding. There is nothing wrong in it. Some how, it worked in the past.

In today's world of numerous progress, and advancements, something far better and beneficial would help. Essentially, it would be without affecting the core faith and values.

Most importantly, those good souls, who still believe in to succeed using profound older ways. In fact, would lose more than they might think. They could hurt their own progress, happiness, and diminish their own beloved God's - Rich Blessings. These very good souls, by reasonably not adapting, would hurdle their faith. Further, unfavorably and considerably hinder their Tangible blessings and benefits that they could blissfully relish.

This hurdle is Not just be for themselves, and also for all around them they care for.

Even though it looks simple, it would be a very hard to sell. This is because, for hundreds and thousands of years, this is how it was considered to be faithful.

In fact, for peace, most of the Good Souls interpreted it correctly. Further, used it in mutually fruitful, and the Appropriate ways.

Those misunderstood, even Good Souls, unfortunately, did harm to all involved. They considered it as sacrilege to "Respect", "Accept" or even "hear about" anything related to other beliefs. Further undesirably, considered it as punishable immorality, and regrettably also involved in harmful deeds. They hurt all they cared for.

It is Sad! It Could Be Avoided. In fact, it is not just only their fault. It's the Ambiguity that is presented to them. They interpreted it wrongfully, and involve in punishable harmful deeds. Now, because the harm caused, they and all they stood for, should sadly suffer.

All the hurt started simply. In the end, not just them but all around them, should go through this completely avoidable, immense sufferings.

To start with, it is about the appropriate use of, more truly divine and beneficial words. We want to rephrase rather wisely and beneficially, of saying, "This is the ONLY". For example, like, **"I believe in my God and I follow my Religion that gives me great meaning and pleasure! At the same time, I Respect your God and Religion, for harmony and peace among us!"**.

This is an example. There could be more profound, agreeable and friendly use of it. That could significantly bring us together, and greatly enrich, not one faith or group, but all.

It might take substantial efforts to implement such and similar simple solutions. But it would greatly bring harmony and pleasure for all faiths and ideas.

Please Notice that, here we are not compelling anyone to strictly follow something. Also, that they do not recognize or may consider sacrilege. We are requesting all to, be courteous, be considerate, and be mutually respectful to other beliefs. Further, proceed peacefully and cheerfully, and follow the fullest of own beliefs. It would be, more comforting and bring more prosperity, for one and all.

When looked deeply, such even simple tolerance, can avoid waste of time, efforts, simply everything. Otherwise, even simple conversation - to start with. But then, even unintentionally, become unwanted quarrels. When intense, might dangerously end in terrible, tragic, and complete destruction. All bad could be avoided!

We radiate peace and prosper, when a difference does not bother us. Especially, if we are able to explicitly respect through agreeable and comforting words. At such circumstances, reasonable and sustainable Common peace and Common Good extends - True Happiness. We All get great opportunity to progress, be in peace, and relish more flourishing pleasures.

More importantly, we would get plenty more opportunities for growth. It would be through content, ease, mutual prosper, and consistent contribution to our own beliefs.

When deeply analyzed, it would offer, a divinely blissful growth. Most Importantly, All the faiths, beliefs and groups, can mutually and respectfully, Not just co-exist, but Sustainably and Peacefully Grow.

Second of all, Profound Ideas need to be enriched. More Reasonable Goodness, need to be interpreted and made explicit, to sensibly protect the vast learning. At the same time, ambiguous and extreme approach towards faiths and beliefs need to be streamlined. This would enhance the harmony. The benefits, ideas, and practices need to be introduced with complete reasoning. Plausibly, it is to be offered from early stage, in simple, joyful ways.

Various beliefs were created hundreds and thousands of years ago. I hope, then, they had only complete goodness as their motivation and inspiration. With all good intention, they had to use the methods, applicable and practiced, during that era.

For various motivations, since then until now, countless interpretations could have been made. These changes might be, to the core original core inception of Complete Goodness.

With the divine blessings and without sacrilege, we need to interpret again. We need help from profound souls of various faiths. We need to create sensible frameworks. It would add more reasonable goodness from their beliefs, to amiably sustain, prosper, and grow.

Guidance could be received from some of the harmonious Great Souls, from all beliefs and practices. Especially, who believe in common Goodness, Sustainable progress, and importantly Completely Reasonable. In brief, this would be an attempt to Help All. Not simple. But I believe, it must be definitely possible by the God's Grace and Blessing.

Whatever bad happened in the past, could not be changed. Only console reasonably and must strive to move on. At least moving forward, agreeable and fruitful changes are must. Particularly, in the past a few Decades, things have changed drastically. Stabilization of the profound and meaningful beliefs is must to reassure, preserve, and thrive sustainably.

The common and powerful beliefs, such as God to be carefully Simplified, Interpreted, and made available. This would be towards common Good without sacrilege. Current and future generations, need to be helped, in the understanding and practices. This is not easy, but we need to start somewhere Reasonable - The sooner the better!

The best approach and implementation of this could produce great results, reliable future, and dependable harmony. This would be for Common Good, in the gradually more informed world, for their own belief's Progress.

We need help from, thoughtful Leaders, Preachers, Gurus and Great Souls from all beliefs. They must be informed on the true benefits. So that they could understand, it is the best for their own beliefs. It's sustainable future, lasting peace and pleasure.

Complete Peace - The Best Way for more cheerful and meaningful future for All!

Religious and such considerable scripts have been interpreted many times. Consciously, they need to be Interpreted a few more times with conscience, genuine reasoning and complete goodness in mind.

It would be Peace, Goodness and Happiness for ALL, with the Divine's blessings.

Thirdly, every Good Soul that believes in God or such beliefs would do more Good. Plausibly, do more Reasonable Good that help and encourage people of all walks of life.

They could promote the Goodness in their own beliefs, through more tangible common Good deeds that they could verify.

Where feasible, they might reasonably, demote the commonly perceived bad aspects from their own beliefs. More importantly, replace and Promote it, with greater beneficial aspects from their own beliefs. This could be a Great favor, for their beloved beliefs and bring great self content and positive results.

Among the various solutions, these steps and recommendations would compliment each other. It would resolve with great results. It would help all beliefs grow progressively, enrich beneficially, and bring peace harmoniously for the entirety.

Additionally, some small portions of self-centered harmful souls might need to be identified, and helped appropriately. A respectful, beneficial and friendly attitude would thrive with them.

They should be helped with Complete Respect, Goodness, and Blessings from their own beliefs. For Happier and Sustainable better Success alternates to be offered. It would be the best to make sure, tangible mutual benefits are produced at each level.

Moreover, it would greatly help that their common Good beliefs to be respected. Where reasonable to be accepted. This would make them truly happy, and they would appreciate profoundly. It could sincerely assist them to become more open minded and supportive.

Through various favorable such steps, they could rationally understand the benefits of openness. Also benefits of Respect towards other beliefs. Initially it might not be easy. But reasonably, it could become easier over time.

Then it would be easy to introduce them to more meaningful thoughts, like,

"Your God knows every single thought, word, deed, and consequences caused. So Think and do Good to save yourself. Be more Blessed and Happier".

"True Prayer is True Love for all souls. So pray also for Common Good. Receive more benefits, as everyone else, will also pray for you". These are just examples. I believe, more such peacemaking and profound thoughts could bring cordial pleasure for all.

All these steps mentioned above will greatly and naturally assist all. Mainly, it would help those who need it the most. Also particularly, who can in turn, help in the overall process of - Peace and Harmony for all.

It might not be simple at all. But in the end, it would be very well worth it - Incredibly!

Sure, the world will all be with full of Blissful-Happiness - with the Blessings of the Divine God!

What if I do not believe in God?

Personally for me, believing in God brings numerous Good opportunities. That positively can be used for Greater Common Good and self Content.

Sometimes, I used to suspect, if can there be God, when reasonably and knowingly, Good people suffer. Also bad people, visibly enjoy all pleasures the world to offer. But, when I thoughtfully analyze and assess it is clear for now. All the Goodness and Happiness that concepts like Soul, God, Religion, Prayer bring, definitely exceeds what the doubts bring.

It brings immense pleasure for me, non-materially. I try to be a profoundly humble, at the same time Reasonable and Sustainable - Goodness based believer!

If you don't believe in God, it is not the worst. Leave the unreasonable fear mongers!

No one exactly knows and proved, what happens for every Soul, when we live, and after death. If truly, there is reasonable Good God, he/she/it, would only produce more Good.

God would truly bless the children - all the creations - All that we could ever conceive.

If question arise, you will get your chance. God as the creator of everyone and everything would forgive you as well, like others. Provided, as long as, you are a reasonable good soul.

If you will, your own value or however you call it - try to keep it as best as you can. With it, rationally produce the most beneficial goodness - in this materialistic world.

In fact, it's assumed by many Good Souls that some who identify themselves as non believers. Who not believe in God or such profound ideas, think more about God. More importantly, they also try to be more ethical people than some so called believers but fakes. They forget God when leaving the prayer hall, and do their usual nasty stuff. I hope these Fakes of yesterday, become Blessed of today. Who knows, you could be one of Good Souls. Who produce the more needful Good that God would truly love. We wish the Best for you!

Just make sure to respect your being here with everyone and everything around you. Be thankful for the everyday help that you receive from them. Do whatever the Good favor you can, for the world that you live in, as a Good fellow being.

Simply, like you say, "Thank you".

I personally identify myself as a spiritual individual, who with respect, analyzes, accepts and follows - Goodness. It is any and all the Goodness from anywhere.

Everyday, I pray the God that I know. I deeply and sincerely pray for Harmony, Goodness and Happiness for all. In simple, I am a believer of the concept God. More importantly, with respect to the Goodness, that could be produced based on that belief - as a Good human being.

Among numerous profound benefits, through this belief, I get opportunity to Thank God. It's without much materialistic involved. I Thank God from my deep heart, for all that I have received, regardless of how little or much.

It makes me feel more content and well even-minded. It feels so wonderful, when I am able to Thank and Appreciate someone or something - beyond myself. Apparently, I do not even know completely, but only rationally.

For instance, **the respect and prayers teach, slowly and steadily that, "It's not Me!", but "It's indescribably Profound and Beyond, that I cannot even imagine!". It naturally and deeply could reduce the "I", "Me", "Mine" - Ego. When it is done in the correct way, it makes the inner Soul more eternal and more at peace.**

I believe, it completes the reasonable - Receive, Enjoy, and Be Thankful - simple at the same time meaningful cycle. With minimal efforts, it makes me at ease, peace, and please.

If something else is Good for you, so be it. I wish you enjoy and follow it. Also rationally you help others enjoy and follow their own beliefs. Provided, in parallel, you are spreading peace, and producing sensible goodness along.

Let us make sure that whatever are our beliefs and differences. We still can help, appreciate, learn, and comfort each other, for the mutual betterment and happiness.

With God's blessings, let us all flourish with complete Goodness and Happiness.

Please note that, when we pray for All, that apparently and profoundly includes us. Especially, it includes those who can bring more joy for us. So, whoever we are, and whatever our current Happiness is.

Let us hope and pray that we all would be Happier with the Blissfulness this world and beyond to offer!

Let's pray for, God bless all of us!

Thank you once again, for your brief journey with me!

Have a Great Day - Every Day!

www.ingramcontent.com/pod-product-compliance
Lightning Source LLC
LaVergne TN
LVHW051020080826
845145LV00009B/2718

* 9 7 8 1 7 3 4 8 2 5 3 4 3 *